# Secrets Behind the
## Customer Experience Shift

# Secrets Behind the
## Customer Experience Shift

Why thoughtful, intentional service
creates unshakeable loyalty

CHARLIE STANLEY

 POWERFUL

**Secrets Behind the Customer Experience Shift**
Why Thoughtful, Intentional Service Creates Unshakeable Loyalty

ISBN: 978-1-78324-357-0 (paperback)
ISBN: 978-1-78324-358-7 (ebook)

Published by Wordzworth.com

This is a work of fiction inspired by real experiences. Names,
characters, organizations, places, events, and incidents are
either products of the author's imagination or used fictitiously.
Any resemblance to actual persons, living or dead, or actual
events is purely coincidental.

For more information, visit https://www.powerfulweb.com/

To Michael Confalone
*Simply put, world-class, my friend.*

# Foreword

There are some people who leave a lasting mark wherever they go; people who don't just do a job but elevate the work, the people around them, and the entire culture of an organization. Michael Confalone is one of those people.

For over two years, I had the privilege of working alongside Michael and watching him grow from someone new to web technology into one of the most trusted, knowledge-able, and beloved members of our team. He didn't just learn the job, he mastered it. From content migration to support, training, and advanced integrations, he became the go-to expert for both our clients and our internal team.

But what truly set Michael apart wasn't just his techni-cal skill. It was his thoughtfulness, his kindness, and his relentless commitment to doing things the right way. He never saw customers as just another support ticket. He saw them as people who deserved to be heard, respected, and cared for. Whether he was helping a client through a difficult issue, training a new team member, or creating a

Loom video to explain something in plain, simple terms, Michael's approach was always the same: make things easier for people, not harder.

His impact wasn't just felt, it was deeply valued. Michael was a cornerstone of our team, a dependable resource, and a friendly face to so many. His ability to tackle challenges, deliver thoughtful solutions, and make people feel truly taken care of set a standard that will influence how we serve customers for years to come.

Michael's legacy within our team lives on, not just in the work he did, but in the standard he set. His approach to thoughtful, intentional service is at the heart of what this book is about. He didn't just solve problems, he created experiences that people remembered.

This book isn't just about customer service. It's about the shift that happens when we stop seeing service as a transaction and start seeing it as an opportunity to connect, build trust, and create loyalty that lasts. It's about taking ownership, leading with kindness, and always striving for excellence.

That's what Michael did every day.
That's what this book is all about.

Kenneth Kimbrell

# Contents

# A Story of Client Experience, Kindness, and Legacy

*Inspired by a Real Standard*

This is a **fictional book, filled with fictional characters.**

But the inspiration behind it? **That's very real.**

At Powerful, we've always placed **client satisfaction at the heart of everything we do.** We want to be **refreshingly different**; a company that doesn't just solve problems but creates lasting relationships, one thoughtful interaction at a time.

And for nearly three years, **Michael Confalone helped make that vision a reality.**

Michael wasn't just a technical support specialist. **He set the standard.**

So much so that, even now, in hiring interviews, our leadership team finds ourselves saying, *"Is this person up to the Michael Standard?"*

It was never an **official metric.** Never something written down.

But through his **kindness, patience, and relentless dedication to doing things the right way,** Michael created something bigger than just his role.

When Michael decided to move on from Powerful, it caught us by surprise. He had been such a core part of our team, and we weren't ready to say goodbye. But he had a deep passion for teaching music, and when an opportunity came for him to follow that passion, he **chose to go after it.**

And while we miss working with him, we're grateful. Grateful that we got to be part of that chapter in his life. Grateful that he got to be part of ours.

This book exists because **Michael's impact on our team was too great not to share.**

It's meant to inspire people to take care of the customer, the client, the fan; to go beyond checking the box and instead make a lasting impression. To be thoughtful. To be kind. To do it right.

That's what we aspire to be. **We aspire to be like Michael.**

While no one can replace him, our hope is that his legacy will continue to shape the way we show up for our clients every day.

So, **cheers to Michael and his new adventure.**

And to you, the reader: I hope you find inspiration in these pages. I hope Riley's journey reminds you of the rare but powerful **kindness, genuineness, and ownership** that make great client relationships possible.

Because in a world where we're so often put on hold, transferred around, and minimized; we have the opportunity to be something better.

Michael showed us how. And now, it's our turn.

**Enjoy the read.**

# CHAPTER 1

# **Welcome Wednesdays**

*A Company That Doesn't
Know What It Wants to Be*

Riley stepped into the lobby of CivicForce, gripping his travel mug like it was the last solid thing in the room.

Immediately, his senses were under attack.

The fluorescent lights buzzed overhead, giving the place a stale, artificial glow. But that wasn't what made him pause.

It was the decor.

The walls, if you could even call them that, were covered in eye-searing primary colors like a kindergarten classroom had been thrown into a blender. Bright red. Neon green. Cartoonish blues.

A massive poster hung over the front desk, screaming:

"WORK HARD, PLAY HARDER!"

Underneath, a stock image of smiling twenty-somethings clinking beer glasses looked eerily photoshopped. And then there was the sign.

"FREE BEER ON TAP IN THE BREAKROOM!"

Riley blinked.

He had worked plenty of jobs. Some had tried to offer "cool" perks, the occasional free snack, a ping-pong table no one had time to use.

But free beer?

This wasn't some laid-back startup.

This was a tech company that burned through employees so fast they were trying to buy their loyalty with alcohol.

What was next? A pizza party to make up for unpaid overtime? The receptionist barely glanced up as Riley walked in. "You're here for Welcome Wednesday?" she asked, her tone flat and detached, like she had asked it a hundred times before.

Riley nodded.

She gestured toward the glass-walled conference room without looking up. "Right through there."

Then, with a quick tap on her headset, she shifted seamlessly back into her conversation as if Riley had already disappeared.

Riley let out a slow breath and stepped inside.

If the lobby had been bad, the conference room was worse.

It looked like someone had designed an "edgy" startup office, then let a group of high schoolers make the final design decisions.

The walls were a chaotic blend of colors, like an elementary school classroom designed by someone who had never met an actual child. The furniture? Cheap plastic, the kind that made an awkward squeak every time someone shifted in their seat.

At the front of the room, a giant screen displayed a PowerPoint: "At CivicForce, We Don't Just Build Websites— We Build the Future of Local Government!"

A stock photo of a smiling city council meeting accompanied the words, making it impossible to tell if this was a tech company or a mandatory community service program.

Seated at the long, white conference table, twelve new hires sat in neat rows.

But Riley noticed something immediately.

Half of them looked like him—mid-career professionals, quiet, scanning the room, already skeptical.

The other half? College kids. They wore CivicForce-branded hoodies, backpacks slouched at their feet. They leaned forward, nodding along too eagerly, their faces lit up like they were about to start the best job ever.

Riley caught snippets of their conversations.

"Dude, they have beer on tap. Like, in the office."

"I heard the fastest reps get cash bonuses."

"Yeah, man, it's all about speed."

Riley exhaled slowly.

He had seen this before.

These weren't just new hires. They were hype men—people who had been sucked into the culture, buying into the speed game, the competition, the chaos.

People who didn't care about helping customers.

They just wanted to win.

Next to Riley, a tall, sharp-eyed man in his early thirties let out a quiet chuckle.

"You know they do this every week, right?"

Riley turned his head. "What?"

"This whole onboarding thing." The guy smirked. "Every Wednesday. We lose people so fast that there's always a new batch coming in."

Riley frowned. "You're kidding."

"I wish." The guy flipped his onboarding packet closed and stretched. "Welcome Wednesday. A CivicForce tradition."

Riley glanced around the room again.

The too-bright walls. The cheap, flimsy furniture. The stock photo smiles on the slides.

It all clicked into place.

High turnover.

That meant something was deeply wrong.

The guy held out his hand. "Jeremy."

Riley shook it. "Riley."

Jeremy smirked. "Let's see if we make it six months."

Tim, the CivicForce onboarding trainer, stood at the front of the room with the rigid posture of someone who had long since perfected the art of fake enthusiasm. He wore a company-branded polo, tucked a little too neatly into his jeans, giving him the look of a man who had fully embraced the corporate script. His expression was carefully measured—a wide, overly practiced smile that never quite reached his eyes.

He had the air of someone who had been doing this for far too long, yet somehow still acted like every onboarding session was the most exciting thing in the world. His voice carried that theme park tour guide energy, the kind of forced cheerfulness that suggested he had repeated this exact presentation dozens, maybe hundreds, of times. He wasn't here to welcome them, he was here to keep the machine running, to shuffle in the next batch of hires, just like he had the last, and just like he would the week after.

Tim clapped his hands, snapping the room's attention back.

"Alright! Let's go around the room and introduce ourselves! Tell us your name, where you're from, and what excites you most about working at CivicForce!"

Jeremy exhaled slowly, muttering, "Oh, this should be good."

The first person, a college-aged guy in a CivicForce hoodie, grinned.

"Hey, I'm Kaleb, and I'm pumped to be here! I love working in fast-paced environments, and I'm stoked to crush some support tickets!"

Tim nodded enthusiastically. "That's the spirit, Kaleb!"

Next was another hoodie-wearing guy.

"Yo, I'm Milo, and I'm just hyped that we can drink on the job."

The college hires laughed.

Riley didn't.

Then came Amber. She looked nervous, but genuinely hopeful.

"Um, hi, I'm Amber. I just moved here from Denver. I was working in IT support before this, and I'm just... excited to be in a role where I can help people."

Tim beamed. "That's great, Amber! Helping people is what we're all about here!"

Jeremy barely concealed an eye roll.

One by one, the new hires introduced themselves. Ethan, Hunter, Tiffany, Emma, Jessie. They came from all over, mostly from other tech companies or customer support roles, looking for something different.

Riley almost laughed.

They had no idea what they had just walked into.

Finally, it was Riley's turn.

"Riley, from Salt Lake City," he said. "Worked in support for a while. Just looking for a place where I can do good work and not burn out."

Tim nodded enthusiastically. "Well, you came to the right place!"

Jeremy barely hid his laugh.

Riley wasn't convinced.

Tim clicked to the next slide, launching into yet another overly rehearsed spiel about CivicForce's "commitment to innovation." Riley let his eyes drift over the room, trying to gauge the mood.

The college hires were still fully engaged, nodding along, completely buying into the hype. They were the ones who would throw themselves into the ticket-closing race, the ones who would drink the beer, chase the bonuses, and brag about their response times.

The rest?

The skeptical veterans, like Jeremy and Riley, had already started to check out.

Riley let his fingers drum lightly against the table, trying to mentally prepare himself for whatever came next.

"Alright, let's move on to something fun!" Tim announced, clicking to a brightly colored slide with confetti graphics.

Riley resisted the urge to roll his eyes.

Tim beamed, clearly excited about this part of the presentation. "Now, CivicForce believes in creating a work environment that is both productive and enjoyable. We understand that our employees work hard, so we make sure you can play hard, too!"

Oh no.

A new slide appeared, plastered with cheesy stock images

of smiling employees high-fiving in open-plan offices.

"Let's talk about the incredible benefits of working here!" Tim continued.

- Free beer on tap in the breakroom!
- A fully stocked snack bar!
- Casual dress code!
- Quarterly pizza parties!

A few of the college hires lit up, exchanging grins and impressed nods.

"Wait, we really get free beer?" one of them—Kaleb, Riley thought—asked.

"Yep!" Tim grinned. "The kegs are refilled twice a week. Just another way we like to reward our hard-working team!"

Jeremy let out a quiet snort.

Riley sighed. He had suspected it before, but now he was sure.

CivicForce wasn't a company invested in its employees.

It was a frat house disguised as a tech company.

The so-called perks were nothing more than cheap distractions, the kind of bare-minimum gestures companies made to keep employees from realizing how miserable they actually were.

Jeremy leaned over. "Notice what's missing?"

Riley glanced at the slide again. It was obvious.

"No mention of raises, career growth, or actual work-life balance."

Jeremy smirked. "Exactly."

Tim, oblivious to the growing skepticism, clicked forward to the next section.

"And now, let's talk about performance expectations!"

A new chart popped up.

- Tickets Resolved Per Hour – Goal: 22
- Average Response Time – Goal: Under 4 minutes
- Customer Satisfaction Score – Optional, but good to have!

Jeremy nudged Riley. "Notice how customer satisfaction is at the bottom?"

Riley exhaled. Throughput was the only thing that mattered here.

Tim continued, his voice brimming with excitement.

"Our top-performing reps clear 27+ tickets per hour! And let me tell you, those who excel can expect some awesome rewards."

Another slide:

- Gift cards for the highest performers!
- Spot bonuses for the fastest response times!
- Leaderboards updated weekly!

At the mention of leaderboards, Milo and a few other younger hires perked up.

Riley could already see it.

They'd turn support into a competition. They'd race to close tickets, caring more about rankings than actual customer service. And management? They'd love it. Because it wasn't about helping clients. It was about speed. Efficiency. Throughput.

Riley had worked places like this before.

And he knew exactly how it ended.

After what felt like an eternity of slides, the onboarding session finally broke for lunch. The group shuffled into the breakroom, which, unsurprisingly, was as tacky as the rest of the office.

A ping-pong table sat in the corner, covered in dust. A half-empty snack bar with bulk Sam's Club-brand chips stood against the wall. And, of course, the beer taps.

Several of the college hires made a beeline for it.

Milo filled a glass, taking a dramatic sip before grinning. "Dude, this is awesome."

Noah, another college hire, laughed. "No kidding. Where else can you get paid to drink on the job?"

Jeremy, watching the scene unfold, let out a dry chuckle.

"They really got you, huh?" he said, shaking his head.

Noah frowned. "What's that supposed to mean?"

Jeremy gestured around the room. "This whole 'culture' thing? It's smoke and mirrors. The beer, the ping-pong table, the leaderboards—it's a distraction."

Noah looked unconvinced. "Man, if you're fast enough, you can make some serious money. The bonuses are insane."

Jeremy smirked. "Yeah? And how long do you think you can keep that up? Six months? A year? What happens when you burn out?"

Noah rolled his eyes. "You just gotta be built different."

Jeremy let out a low laugh and turned to Riley. "You see what we're up against?"

Riley took in the room.

Half the employees were already lost, fully drinking the Kool-Aid. The other half?

They were like him.

Watching. Waiting.

Trying to figure out how long they'd last.

Jeremy sighed. "You wanna know what's really gonna happen?"

Noah, now annoyed, crossed his arms. "Sure, enlighten me."

Jeremy leaned in. "You're gonna grind as hard as you can, stacking up your numbers, chasing those weekly bonuses. But at some point, the stress is gonna get to you. Maybe you have an off week. Maybe your numbers slip. And suddenly, you're not the golden boy anymore."

Noah scoffed, but Jeremy kept going.

"And when that happens? You know what CivicForce does?"

Noah shrugged. "I dunno, coaching session?"

Jeremy smiled. "Nah. They replace you."

Silence.

For the first time, Noah looked uncertain.

Milo, standing beside him, frowned. "That's not how they described it in onboarding."

Jeremy laughed. "Yeah, and every company calls their employees 'family'—right up until they lay you off over email."

As Riley watched the conversation unfold, he felt something settle inside him.

This was not a job built for long-term careers.

It was a grindhouse.

A machine designed to chew through employees, push them to their breaking point, and replace them with fresh hires before they could complain.

Jeremy had seen it.

Riley was starting to see it.

And Noah? Noah still wanted to believe.

But Riley knew one thing for certain. Give it a few months. Noah would figure it out, too. It was the same illusion every bad job sold.

And in a place like this? That illusion wouldn't last. Maybe a few months. Maybe less. Eventually, the grind would catch up to him. Eventually, he'd start seeing what Riley and Jeremy already saw.

Eventually, he'd realize the game was rigged. Noah just didn't know it yet. And right now? He didn't want to.

The group had scattered across the breakroom, grabbing pre-packaged sandwiches from a company fridge that was only half-stocked.

The college hires were still laughing near the beer tap, sipping from company-branded pint glasses like they were out at a bar instead of at work.

Riley, Jeremy, Milo, and Noah took a seat at a corner table, away from the chaos.

Jeremy unwrapped his sandwich with the enthusiasm of someone preparing for execution.

"Noah," Jeremy said, keeping his voice even, "who's the longest-standing employee you've met today?"

Noah frowned. "I mean... Tim, probably?"

Jeremy let out a low chuckle. "Tim's not support, man. Tim's the onboarding guy. He doesn't count."

Milo was starting to catch on. "Wait... are you saying there's no one in support who's been here long-term?"

Jeremy gestured vaguely toward the group of hoodie-wearing college hires still hovering by the beer tap.

"Look at them," he said. "All fresh faces. All hyped up. Ready to crush tickets. But you know what's missing?"

Noah crossed his arms. "What?"

"Anyone who's been here longer than a year."

Silence.

Riley let it settle.

Because Jeremy was right.

Everyone in that onboarding room had been brand new. No senior reps. No tenured employees. No mentors. No one who had lasted.

Milo shifted uncomfortably. "That's... weird."

Tim reappeared in the breakroom, his trademark artificial enthusiasm still going strong.

"Hey guys!" he said, clapping his hands together. "Just wanted to remind you we're jumping back in at 1:30! Got some awesome material on best practices for handling customer requests."

Noah perked up. "Oh, nice—so we're getting trained on troubleshooting?"

Tim blinked, caught off guard.

"Ah—well, no," he said quickly. "Support agents don't really troubleshoot directly. That's what engineering is for."

Noah frowned. "Wait... so what do we do?"

Tim beamed. "You'll be learning how to efficiently direct customers to the right resources!"

Jeremy leaned over to Riley. "Translation: Copy-paste links until the customer gives up."

Riley stifled a laugh.

Noah, to his credit, looked uneasy. "But... what if the articles don't solve the problem?"

Tim smiled wider, as if Noah had just said something adorable.

"That's why we encourage customers to submit tickets for higher-level issues! That way, our engineering team can focus on innovation while we handle the volume."

Jeremy nodded sagely. "Right, right. Because engineering is too important to help customers. Makes total sense."

Tim, pretending not to hear that, checked his watch. "Alright! See you guys back in the conference room!"

As he walked away, Noah rubbed the back of his neck, staring down at the table.

Milo nudged him. "So... still think this place is gonna be different?"

Noah didn't answer.

Riley didn't push it.

Because he already knew the answer.

The rest of onboarding was exactly what Riley expected.

- How to "handle" frustrated customers = How to redirect them until they stop asking for real help.

- How to "engage efficiently" = Copy-paste responses to hit speed metrics.

- How to "manage workload" = Close as many tickets as possible, regardless of whether the issue is actually solved.

By the time they wrapped up, Riley felt like he had been sitting through a bad infomercial for eight hours straight.

Jeremy, as they left the conference room, let out a long sigh.

"Well," he said, stretching, "that was about as soul-crushing as I expected."

Noah was quiet.

Milo was even quieter.

Riley?

He was already thinking about what came next.

He wasn't quitting tomorrow. Not yet. But he wasn't going to waste time here, either. He'd play the game just long enough to figure out his next move. Because if there was one thing he knew for certain...

CivicForce was a dead end.

And Riley didn't plan on sticking around long enough to hit the wall.

# CHAPTER 2

# Numbers Over People

*Another Day in the Queue*

The low hum of fluorescent lights filled the CivicForce office, buzzing just slightly too loud, like an annoying whisper Riley couldn't quite tune out. Rows of desks stretched across the open floor, each occupied by a support agent staring at their screens, typing rapid-fire responses into the queue. The rhythmic clatter of keyboards and occasional dings from chat notifications created a never-ending soundtrack of urgency.

Riley adjusted his headset and clicked "Next Ticket" on his screen.

His monitor refreshed, and a new request appeared.

- Subject: Need Help Updating Council Meeting Minutes
- From: City of Hawthorne Clerk's Office
- Urgency: Low

The request was straightforward. The city clerk couldn't upload PDFs to their document center and needed help troubleshooting. Riley's fingers flew across the keyboard as he checked the system logs.

User error.

She had saved the file in the wrong format, and the upload tool rejected it. A quick response with a link to the Help Center article would solve the problem.

Without thinking, Riley pasted in the standard template:

Hi there! Thanks for reaching out. It looks like your file may be in an incompatible format. Try saving as a standard PDF and re-uploading. Here's a link to our Help Center guide: [Insert Link]. Let us know if you need anything else!

He clicked Send and immediately marked the ticket Resolved.

A second later, a ding sounded in his earpiece.

"Nice work," his manager, Eric, said through the team chat. "Let's keep those resolution times low, Riley. Speed is key."

Riley exhaled.

It was the same reminder Eric had given him every day since he started. Speed is key. Close tickets fast. Keep it moving.

But something about today made the words sit heavier in his chest.

Every morning, Riley and his team received a performance dashboard that tracked their stats in real time.

- Tickets Resolved Per Hour – Goal: 22
- Average Response Time – Goal: Under 4 minutes
- Customer Satisfaction Score – Tracked, but mostly ignored unless it dropped too low

The message was clear:

Close tickets. Do it fast. Move on.

Every time Riley hit Send, his "Resolution Per Hour" score ticked up. His rank shifted on the leaderboard, which was visible to the entire support team. At the top of the list, again; was Callie, one of the fastest reps. She was clearing 25+ tickets per hour, making her a rockstar in Eric's eyes.

But Riley had figured something out.

Callie wasn't actually solving anything.

She pushed tickets along; copying and pasting Help Center links, marking issues as "Resolved" before the client confirmed the fix, and redirecting customers instead of actually fixing problems.

And CivicForce rewarded that.

Riley glanced at the clock. 6:07 PM. Almost time to log out. Just a few more tickets.

Then, a chat request popped up in his queue.

"Hey, I need help updating outage alerts on our homepage. It's not showing the latest information."

Riley opened the admin panel for Cascade Electric's site. He checked the alert system settings and immediately spotted the issue.

A simple caching error.

It was an easy fix, something he could correct in under two minutes.

He cracked his knuckles and prepared to update the settings. Then he stopped.

The CivicForce handbook was clear: Support Agents do not troubleshoot. Clients must submit tickets for advanced issues.

Riley clenched his jaw. It was right there. The solution. Two minutes. But instead, he sighed and typed:

"Sure! Here's a link to our help article on updating alerts: [Insert Link]."

A pause. Then Todd replied:

"I've read that. It's still not working. Can you check what's wrong?"

Riley stared at the screen. He could fix this now. Or he could follow the rules.

"I can't troubleshoot directly, but if you submit a ticket through the portal, someone can take a look."

Another pause.

Todd's next message was shorter, colder.

"So... I need to submit a ticket to get real help?"

Riley felt his stomach twist.

"Yes."

A minute later, the chat closed.

Todd never submitted a ticket. And Riley? He got credit for resolving another case. At the end of the day, Eric's voice came through the team chat.

"Great work today, Callie! 902 tickets resolved this week—huge numbers!"

A string of clapping emojis followed.

"And shoutout to Riley, one of our new hires! Already hitting target response times. Keep it up!"

More emojis.

Riley just stared at the screen.

He had closed 887 tickets that week.

But how many people had he actually helped?

As Riley packed up for the day, Jeremy stopped by his desk.

"You okay, man?"

Riley glanced up. "Yeah. Why?"

Jeremy smirked. "Because you've got that look."

"What look?"

"The 'I'm realizing this job isn't what I thought it was' look."

Riley exhaled. "I don't know, man. It's just... the way we do things here. It doesn't sit right."

Jeremy sat down, shaking his head. "Yeah. Because it's messed up."

He tapped Riley's desk. "You ever wonder why we have so much turnover? Why we're here every Wednesday welcoming new people?"

Riley didn't answer. He didn't have to.

Jeremy sighed. "You know what Callie told me my first week? She said, 'This job's easy if you just stop caring.'"

Riley frowned. "I don't want to stop caring."

Jeremy chuckled. "Yeah. That's what I said, too."

He stood up. "Let's see if you're still saying that in six months."

Riley stared at his metrics dashboard, glowing in the dim office light.

- Tickets Resolved Per Hour: 23.8
- Average Response Time: 3.9 minutes
- Customer Satisfaction Score: Not Tracked

CivicForce would say he had a great day.

So why did it feel like he had done absolutely nothing?

He shut down his computer and left the office, a heavy weight settling in his chest.

Something had to change.

# CHAPTER 3

# The Breaking Point

*The Ticket That Changed Everything*

Riley's fingers hovered over his keyboard; the same way they had thousands of times before. His headset felt heavier than usual, pressing down on his skull like a weight he couldn't shake.

The CivicForce support queue blinked in the corner of his screen. Another ticket had landed in his inbox, flashing red. High-priority.

- **Client:** Katherine – City of Laurelhurst
- **Subject:** URGENT: Homepage Not Updating – Critical Road Closure
- **Urgency:** Emergency

His stomach tightened. Emergency tickets weren't common.

He clicked into the request.

"We've had a major accident on Madison Street, one of our busiest roads. A semi flipped, and traffic is completely blocked in both directions. We need to update the homepage with an emergency alert ASAP, but it's not displaying. Thousands of drivers rely on this info, can someone check why the alert isn't showing?"

Riley sat up straighter, his fingers already moving, pulling up the City of Laurelhurst's website admin panel.

This wasn't some minor formatting issue or a client confused about a new feature. This was thousands of people stuck in gridlock, completely unaware of what was happening, because their city's emergency system had failed them.

The problem was obvious within seconds.

The alert system wasn't pushing updates to the homepage due to a caching error.

The fix?

Clear the cache and refresh the system.

Two minutes.

That's all it would take.

Riley cracked his knuckles and prepared to execute the fix; then froze. Company policy.

Support agents do not troubleshoot critical issues directly. All high-priority cases must be escalated through the client portal. His stomach twisted.

He could fix this right now, or he could follow the rules.

His hands hovered over the keyboard, a war raging in his head.

"Come on, man. Just fix it. Two minutes. Nobody will know."

But then he imagined Eric, his supervisor, watching the dashboard, tracking his "Resolution Time" metrics. He pictured the compliance flag on his profile. The automated warning. The uncomfortable coaching session about "policy adherence."

And worst of all, he imagined himself becoming another burned-out support tech, someone who tried to help people the right way and got written up for it.

He let out a long, slow breath. Then he did the thing he never thought he would do. He copied and pasted the company-approved response.

"Hi Katherine, thanks for reaching out. Please submit a request through our online portal, and our team will investigate further."

His fingers felt like lead as he pressed Send. Katherine responded within seconds.

"I don't have time for that. I need this fixed NOW."

Riley's jaw clenched. So do it. Just fix it.

Instead, his fingers typed:

"I understand the urgency. Unfortunately, all emergency requests must go through our escalation process."

Silence. For a long moment, Katherine didn't respond.

Then: "...You're kidding, right?"

Riley could picture it; Katherine, standing in a city office somewhere, probably on the phone with the mayor's office, trying to explain why their emergency alert system wasn't working.

"People are STUCK out there, Riley. We're trying to redirect traffic, but drivers don't know what's happening. We NEED that alert to update. If you can fix it, please, just fix it."

He squeezed his mouse so hard his knuckles turned white.

Two minutes. Two damn minutes. He could hear Jeremy's voice in his head. "You either stop caring, or you leave." For the first time, Riley understood exactly what he meant. He couldn't fix it. Not because he wasn't able to, but because CivicForce had designed the system so that helping people wasn't the priority. Following policy was.

His stomach churned as he typed the words that would haunt him.

"I'm sorry, Katherine. I can't help with this."

Katherine disconnected from the chat. The ticket closed. And Riley felt sick.

Thirty minutes later, Eric's voice crackled in Riley's headset.

"Hey, Riley, got a second?"

Riley exhaled sharply and forced his voice to stay neutral. "Yeah, what's up?"

"Just wanted to say—you did great with that Laurelhurst ticket."

Riley's entire body went rigid. "Excuse me?"

"You stuck to the process," Eric said, completely oblivious. "Didn't let emotions get in the way. That's exactly what we want to see."

Riley's hands curled into fists under his desk.

Thousands of people had been stuck in traffic with no information. Katherine had begged for help. And he was being praised for doing nothing.

He didn't respond. "Anyway," Eric continued, "keep up the good work!"

The call ended. Riley sat there, staring at his screen. Slowly, he took off his headset. Then he closed his laptop. Then he stood up. And he walked out. He wasn't coming back.

That night, Riley sat on his couch, staring at his laptop.

For the first time in years, he felt completely disillusioned with his career. He had gotten into tech support because he liked solving problems, but CivicForce had shown him that some companies don't want problems solved. They wanted compliance. They wanted efficiency.

They wanted a warm body at a desk, answering tickets as fast as possible. He had given them that.

And he hated himself for it. Riley sighed and opened up a job board.

He didn't want another soulless support job. He didn't want another turn-and-burn company that treated customers like numbers.

Then, he saw it.

**Powerful – Web Solutions for Utility Organizations**
Technical Support Specialist – Client-Focused, Long-Term Partnerships

His eyes skimmed the description.

- "We don't just solve issues—we build relationships."
- "We take the time to understand our clients."
- "We believe amazing client satisfaction is a craft, not a checklist."

Riley sat back. It sounded… different. Maybe it was just another company saying what people wanted to hear. Maybe they were full of it. But maybe, just maybe, they weren't.

He clicked Apply.

And for the first time in months, he felt hopeful.

# CHAPTER 4

# A Different Kind of Company

*The Final Interview,*
*A First Impression Like No Other*

Riley had been through a lot of interviews in his career.

Most of them were the same. You walked into a stiff office, sat across from someone in a suit, and answered a series of scripted questions while they barely looked up from their clipboard. There was always a forced politeness, an unspoken power dynamic, like they already knew whether they wanted you before you even shook their hand.

He had expected something similar today.

But this?

This was already different.

The email had given him a conference center address, not an office, which made sense given that Powerful was fully remote. And instead of driving, he had flown in—courtesy of Powerful.

They had booked the flight, the hotel, covered the Uber ride to and from the airport, and even sent him a reimbursement for mileage back home. No company had ever done that for an interview before. It was a small thing, but it sent a clear message: We value your time, and we want this to be a good experience for you, too.

Even with all of that, Riley still felt a little uneasy.

Because it almost seemed too good to be true.

He stepped into the conference room, scanning the space. It was simple—professional but warm. The walls were lined with framed photos of what looked like local landmarks. The table was clean and organized, with a neatly printed agenda and guide placed in front of a chair.

Before he could read it, the door opened, and Jordan walked in, smiling.

"Riley! Great to finally meet you in person."

Riley stood, shaking his hand, still a little unsure how to read the guy. Jordan was dressed professionally—but with a twist.

- Khakis, a crisp white dress shirt.
- A light blue sweater vest with the Powerful logo.
- And... light blue running shoes.

It threw Riley off just enough to notice. Professional, but approachable. Structured, but not stiff.

Jordan gestured toward the table. "Go ahead and set your stuff down," he said, motioning to a chair. "But before we get started, the first thing on our agenda is getting a cup of coffee."

Riley blinked. "Wait, what?"

Jordan chuckled. "Look, I know this is an in-person interview for you, and that can feel formal. But we want to be thoughtful and give you a chance to relax. We've already had our Zoom interview, and you've met some of the team. This? This is just a chance to get to know each other better. A little walk will help calm any nerves and let you be the best version of yourself before we jump into the formal questions."

Riley hesitated. An interview that starts with a walk?

This was not CivicForce.

"Come on," Jordan said, grabbing his jacket. "You like pastries?"

Riley nodded.

"Good," Jordan grinned. "Because we're getting some of those too."

And just like that, they walked out into the brisk morning air. The air was crisp, with a light breeze cutting through the quiet city streets. It was early enough that foot traffic was minimal, and the low hum of distant traffic filled the spaces between their conversation.

Jordan didn't start with work.

"How was your flight?"

"You ever been to Portland before?"

"Got anything fun planned for the weekend?"

Riley was thrown off at first. He had never had an interview like this. Most hiring managers wanted to see how fast you could spit out polished answers, how well you could regurgitate bullet points from your résumé.

But Jordan actually wanted to know him.

As they walked, Riley felt his shoulders start to relax. The rhythm of the conversation was easy, unforced. He found himself answering with more honesty than he had in past interviews.

"It's funny," Riley admitted, "I was pretty skeptical coming into this."

Jordan raised an eyebrow. "Oh yeah?"

"I mean, let's be real. Most companies say they care about culture, about clients, about employees. But then, once you're hired, you're just another cog in the machine. It's all talk."

Jordan nodded, hands in his pockets. "Yeah, I get that. I've worked places like that too. But we don't just say it. We're built for it."

They reached the coffee shop, a small, locally owned place with the kind of charm you only found in cities that took their coffee culture seriously. Riley ordered a black coffee, still processing how different this all felt. Then Jordan added a few pastries to the order.

"For later," he said casually. "Gotta have snacks back in the conference room."

It was such a small thing. But it told Riley everything he needed to know.

Jordan wasn't just checking a box.

Jordan cared.

Back in the conference room, Riley finally got a chance to look at the printed agenda. The first line made him grin.

- Walk to coffee shop

Underneath that, it outlined:

- In-Depth Conversation and Interview
- Team Lunch
- Leadership Chat
- Break and Reflection Time
- Dinner
- Wrap Up

Jordan took a sip of his coffee and smiled. "Alright, let's get into it."

Riley felt calmer now. More himself. And Jordan had done that on purpose.

"So," Jordan said, "we talk a lot about client experience here. A lot of companies say they care about customers, but we mean it. We don't just close tickets, we create relationships. And a lot of that philosophy? It comes from one person."

He leaned forward slightly. "Have you heard about Michael yet?"

Riley frowned. "Michael?"

Jordan grinned. "Oh, you will."

He set his coffee down and laced his fingers together. "Michael is a support legend. Customers love him. Not just because he's good at solving problems, but because he always cared. He always took ownership. He was always relentless about improving the client experience."

Riley could hear the genuine admiration in Jordan's voice.

"We call it the Michael Standard."

Something stirred in Riley. He had spent years working jobs where speed mattered more than care, where efficiency was valued over relationships. He had never met this Michael guy, but he could already tell—this was a different level.

"How am I ever going to live up to this guy?"

Jordan must have sensed the thought. He smiled. "We don't expect you to be Michael. We expect you to be Riley. But we do hope you take inspiration from him."

Riley nodded slowly. He wasn't sure if he could live up to the standard everyone seemed to hold so highly. But for the first time in a long time, he felt something he hadn't felt in years.

Riley sat up a little straighter, shifting his coffee cup between his hands. He had spent years working jobs where speed mattered more than care, where efficiency was valued over relationships. But here? He hadn't even started yet, and he was already feeling the weight of something different. Something purposeful.

Jordan glanced at the agenda. "Alright, next up, the in-depth conversation and interview."

Riley nodded, feeling ready.

Jordan leaned back, his posture relaxed but focused. "Alright, Riley. We've talked about culture, about how we do things differently. Now, let's dig into you. What excites you about this job?"

Riley took a second to think. The easy answer would have been a fresh start or a remote job with a great company, but he knew Jordan wanted something deeper.

"I like solving problems," Riley said finally. "But not just fixing things, I like knowing that I've made something easier for someone. That a client isn't just relieved that an issue is gone, but actually feels taken care of. I haven't always been in places where that mattered."

Jordan nodded approvingly. "And what frustrates you?"

"Being forced to do things the wrong way." Riley surprised himself with how quickly the answer came out. "I've been in places where speed was more important than doing things properly. I don't mind working hard, but I hate when the process gets in the way of actually helping people."

Jordan grinned. "Yeah, you're going to fit in just fine here."

They continued talking, covering everything from how Riley handled difficult customers to how he learned best. But the conversation didn't feel like a test. It felt like a discussion between equals.

At some point, Riley realized he wasn't nervous anymore. He was actually... enjoying this.

Jordan glanced at the time. "Alright, let's continue this over lunch. You ready to meet the team?"

The restaurant was a casual but stylish place not far from the conference center. When they walked in, Riley saw a group of team members in Powerful gear already seated, chatting easily.

"Riley!" A woman with dark curly hair waved him over. "Welcome to the circus!"

Jordan chuckled. "That's Laura, and she's not wrong."

The next few minutes were a blur of handshakes, names, and introductions. Erin, Sean, Mary, and Laura—all from different areas of the company.

Riley had expected a typical corporate lunch, where people made small talk and barely touched their food. Instead, it was laughter, inside jokes, and genuine conversation.

"So, Jordan's been hyping up this Michael guy," Riley said after a while. "What's the deal?"

Laura, a website project manager, grinned. "Oh, you're in for it now."

Sean leaned forward. "Michael's like a myth, a legend. Clients talk about him like he personally saved their utility organization."

"He probably did," Mary added. "He once trained a client's entire team for free because he didn't want them to struggle."

Laura smirked. "Yeah, and the 'Michael Standard' isn't just a saying. It's how we actually evaluate if we're doing things right."

Riley shook his head, laughing. "Okay, now I really have to live up to this guy."

Jordan smiled. "You'll figure out your own way. Just take the inspiration where it fits."

As the plates were cleared, Riley felt something shift. He wasn't just interviewing anymore.

He was already starting to belong.

After lunch, they headed back to the conference center, where Chase one of the members of the senior leadership team at Powerful, was waiting.

Chase was easygoing but sharp, the kind of leader who could make you feel like an old friend but still command a room. He greeted Riley warmly before they sat down.

"So, what do you think so far?" Chase asked.

Riley was honest. "I'm still wrapping my head around it. It's so different from where I've been. But... it feels right."

Chase nodded. "That's what we aim for. Riley, you're not here to be another worker in the system. We don't believe in just doing things because that's how they've always been done. We believe in making experiences better; for our clients, for our team, for everyone."

He leaned forward slightly. "But that takes people who care. People who see their job as a craft, not a checklist. Don't get me wrong, we have checklists; but it's the craft and humanized experience that makes it magical."

The way he said it made something click in Riley's head. This wasn't a company that hired people to fill seats.

This was a company that built something real.

Chase smiled. "I hope you decide to be a part of it."

After his conversation with Chase, Riley was given an hour of quiet time to reflect. It wasn't something he expected, but he was grateful for it.

He took a seat in a quiet lounge area, sipping a coffee, browsing the Powerful core values on his iPhone.

No part of this process had been rushed. Every step had been thoughtful, personal, and intentional.

Riley let that sink in.

He had spent years waiting for a company that actually valued this stuff.

Maybe, just maybe, he had finally found it.

That evening, Jordan took Riley out for a relaxed dinner. By now, the conversation had shifted away from work and into life.

They talked about hobbies, travel, personal goals. Jordan shared stories about past conferences, moments when clients had cried after realizing they were finally being taken care of.

"You don't have to be Michael," Jordan said at one point. "But you're going to leave a mark here. I can already tell."

And for the first time, Riley believed him.

As Riley headed back to his hotel, he felt a mix of exhaustion and excitement.

This wasn't just a job.

This was a chance to do something different.

And as he lay in bed that night, staring at the ceiling, one thought repeated in his mind.

"I think I found the place where I belong."

# CHAPTER 5

# The First Day, A Welcome Like No Other

*Flying in the Right Way*

Riley had expected his first day at Powerful to feel like every other first day he'd had at a new company.

A rushed morning, a stack of paperwork waiting for him, a half-functioning laptop that needed hours of setup. A rushed HR rep handing him a thick company handbook, barely making eye contact before moving on to the next new hire. That was how it always went.

But this?

This was different.

For starters, he didn't even drive in. Powerful flew out to him.

That alone had caught him off guard. A few days before his start date, Jordan had sent him a message.

"Hey Riley, Hannah and I are flying out to your city to welcome you. We've booked a conference center for your first day, so you can settle in somewhere familiar. Everything's taken care of, see you soon!"

That was it. No corporate headquarters, no generic training room filled with plastic chairs, no maze of cubicles to navigate. Just a simple message telling him, We're coming to you.

Riley had never heard of a company doing this before.

It almost felt... unnecessary. But now, as he stepped into the conference room, he realized something.

They weren't just saying they did things differently.

They were showing it. It was a first impression like no other.

The conference room had an air of quiet elegance, with sleek wood-paneled walls and a long table that had been set up just for him. Not just a chair and a laptop, but a full experience.

The smell of fresh coffee and warm pastries filled the air. A tray of croissants, muffins, and fresh fruit sat neatly arranged on the table. The soft hum of the overhead lights gave the room a warm, inviting glow.

And then there was the welcome box.

Riley's name was printed on the front in bold, embossed letters, giving it a personalized touch that made him pause for a second. He hadn't even opened it yet, and already, it felt intentional.

Slowly, he lifted the lid.

Inside was a brand-new laptop, still shrink-wrapped, pre-installed with everything he needed. No hours spent setting up software. No submitting an IT ticket for missing access. It was just... ready.

Beside it was a sealed envelope with his credentials inside. No generic sticky note with a password scribbled on it. The envelope felt official, professional, like it had been planned in advance.

Then he noticed the clothing. A tie that matched Jordan's— custom-designed with the Powerful logo in an Argyle pattern. Matching socks, a polo, a pullover. All of it in Powerful's signature colors, neatly folded.

At the bottom of the box was a leather padfolio, embossed with the Powerful logo. He ran his fingers over the cover, feeling the smooth texture of the leather before flipping it open. Inside was his 90-day plan.

He started skimming the pages, expecting to see something vague, like "Learn company values" or "Shadow team members." Instead, the very first sentence made him stop.

"Your first 90 days aren't about proving yourself. They're about preparing you to succeed."

He exhaled.

This wasn't just a company onboarding process. This was an investment.

"Feels different, doesn't it?"

Riley looked up to see Jordan standing near the doorway, smiling as he poured himself a cup of coffee.

"Yeah," Riley admitted. "It really does."

Jordan walked over, nodding toward the welcome box. "You know, most companies onboard people like they're a liability. We do it differently." He took a sip before continuing. "We don't want employees. We want partners. We want to make sure you're absolutely ready before you ever talk to a client."

Riley's fingers tightened around the pages of his 90-day plan. That was another thing he wasn't used to.

At CivicForce, he had been thrown into the fire immediately. First-day onboarding was nothing more than paperwork, a quick IT setup, and then—bam. Tickets in the queue. Figure it out.

By day three, he was expected to be handling support cases solo. No structured training, no thoughtful introduction to the clients. Just sink or swim.

And now?

Powerful was telling him the opposite.

"We don't rush people here," Jordan said, reading his expression. "We set them up for success."

Riley swallowed. "That's... rare."

Jordan grinned. "Yeah. And that's exactly why we do it."

Riley flipped through a few more pages of his onboarding plan. His schedule for the first few weeks was neatly outlined—structured training sessions, hands-on practice before taking any live client requests, regular check-ins.

Then, near the bottom, he noticed something.

A section labeled "The Michael Standard."

He frowned. "Michael?"

Jordan chuckled. "Oh, you're going to hear that name a lot."

Riley looked up. "Who is he?"

Jordan leaned against the table, crossing his arms. "Michael Confalone. One of the best technical support specialists we ever had. Clients loved him. I mean, *loved him.*"

Riley raised an eyebrow. "Like... how much are we talking?"
Jordan smirked. "You ever seen a client hug their support

rep at a conference?"

Riley blinked. "No. Never."

"Yeah, well, that's the kind of loyalty Michael built."

Riley nodded slowly, flipping back to the first page of his onboarding plan. The words stood out even more now.

"Your first 90 days aren't about proving yourself. They're about preparing you to succeed."

He exhaled again. This was real. This was intentional. This was different.

And once again, that name echoed in his mind. Michael. The legend. The gold standard. The person everyone loved.

And for the first time, it wasn't just intimidating. It was inspiring.

# CHAPTER 6

# Learning to Unlearn

*Discovering Michael's How-To Video Library*

Riley had just finished his morning training session when a new Slack message popped up from Jordan.

Jordan: "Hey Riley—when you have a chance, dig into some of Michael's old videos. He made a ton of them for clients. Should give you a feel for how we approach things here." Riley replied with a thumbs-up emoji, but in his head, he was already intrigued.

Michael. The guy everyone loved. The guy who had somehow set the gold standard for how Powerful treated clients. And now, Riley was about to see him in action. He navigated to the internal knowledge base and found a folder labeled "Michael's Client Videos." There were hundreds. HUNDREDS.

Riley scrolled through the titles, his eyebrows rising.

- How to Update Emergency Alerts
- Fixing Broken Links on Your Homepage
- Adding New Users to Your CMS
- Troubleshooting Outage Notifications

Every single one was a personalized response to a real client's issue. Michael hadn't just answered questions with emails. He had taken the extra step, almost every time, to record a short Loom video, walking the client through the solution like he was sitting right next to them. No wonder people still talked about him. Riley clicked on the first video. Michael's face appeared on screen—mid-20s, warm smile, easygoing energy.

"Hey Melissa! Thanks for reaching out about updating your outage alerts. No worries; this is super simple, and I'll walk you through it step by step."

Riley leaned in. Michael's tone was casual, confident, and kind—like he was talking to a friend, not a client. As Michael shared his screen, he explained each step like a natural teacher, never rushed, never impatient. And then came the part that made Riley pause the video and replay it. And he said, "if you ever forget these steps, no stress. Just rewatch this anytime. You got this!" Riley froze. That was it. That was why clients loved him. Michael wasn't just solving problems. He was giving people confidence. He made them feel capable. Made them feel like they mattered. Riley clicked on another video. Then another. Then another.

He lost track of time. Each video was so simple—yet so powerful.

Michael never talked down to clients.
Never sounded annoyed or frustrated.
Never made them feel like a burden.

Instead, he empowered them. He turned every request into an opportunity to make someone feel valued. Riley sat back in his chair, shaking his head. "This guy is the maestro of creating raving fans." And now? Riley wanted to be just like that.

Riley started taking his first real client requests. And immediately, he struggled. His old CivicForce habits still lingered. His first instinct was always speed. His replies were too short, too clinical. Jordan noticed. So did Kelly.

So did Kyle. But instead of calling him out—they coached him up. Like the first time he sent a perfectly accurate, but kind of cold response. Jordan messaged him: "Hey Riley, great info in that response. But take a sec and think... How would Michael have said this?"

Riley groaned but re-read his own message. It was correct—but it didn't make the client feel anything. He sighed, deleted it, and rewrote it.

"Hey Lisa, thanks for reaching out! No worries, this is an easy fix, and I'll walk you through it. I've attached a quick step-by-step, but if it helps, I can also send a short video.

Let me know what works best for you!"

Send.

A few minutes later, Lisa responded. "Wow, Riley, THANK YOU. This was so clear. Seriously, you just saved me so much time!" Riley exhaled. That was different. And it felt good.

Even though Riley was improving, his old habits still crept in. One afternoon, he found himself rushing through a backlog of tickets, trying to keep up. He sent quick, efficient responses—but they lacked warmth. Then Kyle messaged him: "Hey man, I see you flying through tickets. But remember, quality over quantity, right?" Riley hesitated. Kyle was right. He was slipping back into old patterns. He closed his eyes for a second, then re-opened a ticket. Slowed down. Rewrote his response. Made sure the client felt taken care of. And when he hit Send, he felt something he hadn't felt in a long time. Pride.

That night, Riley sat at his desk, thinking about the how-to videos that Michael made. The tone. The kindness. The intentionality. Michael wasn't older. Michael wasn't some seasoned industry veteran. Michael was just a guy.

A guy who made a choice. He chose to do things differently. Chose to be thoughtful. Chose to empower clients instead of just fixing their problems. And that's why clients loved him. Riley wanted that.

He wanted to be so good, so helpful, so genuine that people lined up at conferences asking for him by name.

He wanted to create raving fans. And now? For the first time, he knew exactly how to do it. He didn't have to be Michael. But he could live up to the Michael Standard. And maybe, just maybe, one day, clients would be saying: "Oh, you work with Powerful? Is Riley still there? That guy was the best."

# CHAPTER 7

# The First Big Test

*The Client: Ryan from Sellwood Electric*

Riley had just settled in for the morning when a high-priority ticket popped into his queue.

- **Client:** Ryan – Sellwood Electric Cooperative
- **Subject:** URGENT: Homepage Outage Map Not Updating
- **Urgency:** Critical

Riley clicked into the ticket and read Ryan's message: "Hey team, we've got storms rolling in, and our outage map isn't updating. We need this fixed ASAP—our customers rely on this for real-time updates. Can someone check what's going on?" Riley's pulse picked up. This was a big deal. Thousands of people were checking Sellwood

Electric's website, trying to see if their power was out—and the data wasn't refreshing. He clicked into the system logs. It was an API issue. The data feed from their internal outage tracking system was failing to sync with their website. It wasn't a complicated fix, but it needed to be handled carefully. Riley's first instinct? Speed. "I need to get this done FAST." His fingers flew to his keyboard; but then, he stopped.

The voice in his head, "Slow Down." Michael's voice echoed in his mind.

"The moment you rush, you stop listening. And the moment you stop listening, you stop helping." Riley exhaled slowly. Don't just fix it. Think about the client. He opened a chat with Ryan.

Riley: "Hey Ryan! I see the issue—it's an API sync problem. I can start working on a fix right now, but I want to check something first. Are you seeing any error messages on your end?"

Ryan replied almost immediately. "No errors, but the timestamps aren't updating. It's still showing last night's outage data." Riley dug deeper into the logs. Yep. The API wasn't failing—it was stuck. The system wasn't pulling new data, but it wasn't throwing an error either. A quick fix would have been resetting the API manually—but that would only be a temporary solution. Riley paused. Think like Michael.

Would Michael just patch it up and move on?

Or would he make sure the client felt taken care of? Riley made a decision.

Riley: "I can reset the API now, but I want to make sure this doesn't happen again. I'm going to adjust the sync timing and set up a failsafe. That way, even if it gets stuck in the future, it'll automatically refresh. Should only take a few extra minutes—does that work for you?"

A pause.

Then Ryan responded: "Wait—you can do that? Dude, YES. That would be amazing."

Riley grinned and got to work. He tweaked the API settings, tested the new sync timing, and added an automatic failover in case the data stalled again. Ten minutes later, he pinged Ryan.

Riley: "All set! The outage map should now update automatically every 60 seconds. And if anything gets stuck, it'll force-refresh after five minutes. You should be good to go."

Ryan's reply came fast: "Riley. YOU. ARE. THE. BEST. Seriously, you just saved us a ton of stress. I owe you a beer at the next conference."

Riley laughed. This wasn't just fixing a problem. This was building trust. For the first time, he understood what Michael had been doing all along.

An hour later, Jordan messaged him, "Hey, saw that Sellwood Electric ticket—Ryan is singing your praises. Awesome job!"

Riley felt a surge of pride.

Jordan continued, "That's what we're about, man. Not just solving problems, creating raving fans."

Riley leaned back in his chair, letting it sink in. This was it. This was what he wanted to do. For the first time in years, Riley felt like he was exactly where he was supposed to be.

# CHAPTER 8

# The First Conference

*San Antonio – A Whole New World*

Riley stepped out of the airport and into the humid, sunlit air of San Antonio. This was his first-ever industry conference. And to be honest? He had no idea what to expect. Back at CivicForce, client relationships had been transactional—contracts, emails, and support tickets. But at Powerful, clients stuck around for years. And today? Riley was about to see what that actually looked like.

The convention center was huge, filled with vendors, speakers, and booths from companies across the industry. Riley followed Jordan toward the Powerful booth, which was already buzzing with activity. A massive Powerful-branded backdrop stood behind the booth, along with a sleek counter filled with giveaways such as branded notebooks, coffee mugs, and socks. But the thing that caught

Riley's eye? An old handwritten sign, taped casually to the side of the booth.

"THE LINE STARTS HERE TO HUG MICHAEL."

Riley stopped in his tracks. "No way." Even here, in Texas, Michael's presence still lingered. Jordan saw Riley staring and smirked. "Told you, man. He's a legend."

Riley had been at the booth for maybe twenty minutes when someone tapped his arm. He turned to see a woman with short, dark hair and a friendly smile. "Wait, you're Riley, right?" she asked. Riley blinked. "Uh… yeah?" She grinned.

"I'm Jenny, from Willamette Valley PUD. You helped me a few weeks ago with that crazy security permissions issue. You probably don't remember." Riley did remember. She had emailed in a panic, her team couldn't access their website admin panel, and it was two hours before a board meeting. She had been stressed, overwhelmed, and worried about disappointing her team.

Riley had taken his time, walked her through the solution, and sent a follow-up just to check in. And now? She was standing here, in Texas, thanking him in person. "Seriously, Riley," Jenny continued, "you saved me that day. And it wasn't just that you fixed the problem, it was how you handled it. You were so patient. I could tell you actually cared."

Riley felt a rush of pride and, if he was honest, a little shock. He had spent years thinking support was invisible work. But here was a client, in another state, remembering his name. Jordan, who had been listening nearby, nudged him. "That's what it's about, man." Riley looked back at Jenny, smiling. "It was my pleasure, really. I'm just glad everything worked out." She laughed. "Worked out? You made me look like a rockstar in front of my whole team. I owe you one." Riley scratched the back of his neck, still a little overwhelmed. "Well, if you ever need anything again, you know where to find me."

Jenny grinned. "Oh, trust me; I'll be asking for you by name."

That night, Riley sat outside the conference center, staring at the city lights reflecting off the river. Today had been a turning point. For the first time, he felt it. This wasn't just a job. It was about trust. Relationships. Long-term impact. People didn't just remember Michael because he was good at technical support. They remembered him because he made them feel valued. And now? Riley was starting to do the same. He didn't have to be Michael. But he could live up to the Michael Standard. And maybe—just maybe—one day, there'd be a new sign at the booth.

"THE LINE STARTS HERE TO HUG RILEY."

The conference was a whirlwind; Riley had been on his feet for hours, shaking hands, answering questions, and getting a crash course in what long-term client relationships looked like. He was still processing what had happened with Jenny from Willamette Valley PUD.

She had remembered him. She had sought him out. She had told him, to his face, that he had made a difference. It was a feeling he wasn't used to. And then it happened again. Late in the afternoon, Riley was helping restock giveaway items at the Powerful booth when he heard someone say his name. "Riley?" He turned to see a woman in her early thirties, curly brown hair pulled into a loose bun, wearing a Sunnyside Water Authority badge. "Hey! I thought that was you!" she said, smiling as she approached. Riley blinked. He recognized her name immediately.

Terra.

They had worked together just last week.

She had reached out about a confusing issue with form submissions on Sunnyside's website. Customers were trying to submit water service requests, but the forms were acting glitchy—some going through, others not.

At first, Riley had assumed it was a bug. But after digging deeper, he realized the problem wasn't technical—it was design-related. Some of Sunnyside's customers weren't completing all required fields because of poor form layout. Most support reps would have fixed the immediate problem and moved on. But Riley had decided to go further. Instead of just patching it up, he had sent Terra a short Loom video, explaining:

"Hey Terra! I fixed the form issue, but I also wanted to flag something—some of your customers might be skipping fields because of the way the layout flows. I mocked up a simpler version that should reduce confusion. No pressure to change it, just wanted to share in case it helps!"

And now? Here she was, standing in front of him in San Antonio, Texas, smiling like they were old friends.

"You didn't have to do that! I just wanted to say thank you," Terra said. "For what?" Riley asked, still caught a little off guard.

"For actually thinking ahead." She shook her head, still smiling. "Most support reps just fix what's broken. But you actually looked for ways to make things better."

Riley chuckled, scratching the back of his neck. "Well... I just figured if I noticed something, I might as well mention it."

Terra gave him a look. "Riley. You mocked up an entire new form layout and sent me a video explaining it. That wasn't just 'mentioning it.' That was going above and beyond." Riley blinked. She was right. At CivicForce, he would have never done that. He would have closed the ticket, moved on. But now? Now, he was starting to think differently.

Terra crossed her arms, shaking her head with a laugh. "You know what's funny?" she said.

"What?"

"After I watched your video, I told my team, 'This guy reminds me of Michael.'" Riley's stomach flipped. "Wait... seriously?"

"Oh yeah," Terra grinned. "I met Michael at this same con-ference a few years ago. The way you explain things, the way you actually care, it reminded me of him."

Riley's mind spun. He had spent weeks hearing about Michael. Watching his old videos. Studying his tone, his approach. Trying to live up to this impossible standard. And now, for the first time...

Someone had said he reminded them of Michael. He felt a slow, growing sense of pride. Maybe he wasn't just learn-ing the Michael Standard. Maybe he was becoming his own version of it. Terra grinned and patted his arm.

"Anyway, just wanted to say thanks. You made my life easier." And just like that, she was gone, off to her next session, blending into the sea of conference attendees. Riley stood there for a long moment, processing what had just happened. Then, from behind him, Jordan chuckled. "That's two today, huh?"

Riley turned to see Jordan leaning against the booth, arms crossed, smirking. "First Jenny, now Terra. People are noticing you, man." Riley let out a breath and shook his head, still a little overwhelmed. "This is... new for me," he admitted. Jordan clapped a hand on his shoulder. "Get used to it."

That night, Riley sat on the balcony of his hotel, looking out over the city. This had been his first-ever industry confer-ence. And already, two different clients had remembered him. Not just because he had fixed something for them. But because he had made them feel taken care of. He glanced down at his conference badge, running his fingers over the Powerful logo.

For the first time, he truly understood what it meant to do this job the right way. Michael had set the bar. And Riley? He was finally stepping up to meet it. Maybe one day, there'd be a new sign at the booth.

"THE LINE STARTS HERE TO HUG RILEY."

And for the first time, that didn't feel impossible. It felt inevitable.

The next morning Riley walked through airport security, shoes in one hand, laptop in the other, still processing everything that had happened at the conference. He had met real clients. Not just names on support tickets, but actual people who remembered him. Who appreciated him. Who trusted him. Jenny. Terra. The Michael Standard. And now, as he grabbed his bag and headed toward his gate, he heard it. "Riley!" He turned, confused; then saw a guy jogging toward him.

Early forties, slightly out of breath, wearing a Cedar Hills Telephone and Broadband polo. Riley recognized him instantly. "Adam?" Adam grinned. "Man, I can't believe I ran into you! I had to say hi." They shook hands, and Adam laughed. "I was at the conference, but I barely made it to anything; got stuck in my hotel room working. But I'm so glad I ran into you now. I've been meaning to say something." Riley raised an eyebrow. "Oh yeah?"

Adam clapped a hand on his shoulder. "I just wanted to thank you, man. I know you've helped me a couple of times, but what you did for Julie? That was above and beyond." Riley frowned for a second. Julie. Then he remembered. Julie was new on Adam's team, a recent hire who had reached out in a panic a few weeks ago when Adam was out sick. She had needed help updating content on their website, but she wasn't comfortable navigating their system yet. Technically, Cedar Hills had not opted into these kind of virtual webmaster updates with Powerful.

But Riley had taken one look at the situation and thought Michael wouldn't just say 'not my job.' So instead of sending Julie away, he had jumped on a call, walked her through it step by step, and even made a short Loom video so she could reference it later. At the time, Riley hadn't thought much of it. But now, standing here in the airport, hearing Adam talk about it like it actually mattered, that felt different.

"Dude," Adam continued, shaking his head. "That's not even a service we use with you guys. But you just stepped up and helped my team when I wasn't there. I can't tell you how much that meant to me." Riley shrugged. "It wasn't a big deal." Adam shook his head, grinning. "No, man. It was. And I just wanted to say thanks. Seriously. You're a rock star." Adam checked his phone and groaned. "I gotta catch my flight to Montana. I know you're heading to Salt Lake. But I just had to stop and say thanks." Then, before walking off, he added something that hit Riley like a freight train. "Thanks for being you." Then he was gone, disappearing into the crowd of travelers. Riley stood there, rooted to the spot, those words echoing in his head. "Thanks for being you." Not thanks for fixing the issue. Not thanks for responding quickly. Not thanks for following the process. Just, "Thanks for being you."

Riley swallowed hard, staring out at the terminal, watching people rush to their gates.

For weeks, he had been chasing Michael's legacy, trying to live up to someone else's reputation. But now? For the first time, he wondered; "Maybe I don't have to be Michael."

"Maybe I just have to be the best version of Riley." And for the first time, That felt like enough.

# CHAPTER 9

# Becoming a Trusted Partner

*The Long-Term Project – Oswego City Light*

Riley's name popped up in a new client assignment.

- Client: Warren Miller, Oswego City Light
- Project: Post-Launch Support & Advanced Features Implementation
- Duration: 4 to 5 Weeks

Riley's eyebrows lifted. This wasn't just a ticket. This was a real project, a long-term support engagement with a single client. And Warren? He wasn't just asking for help. He was relying on Riley to guide him through it.

The next morning, Riley logged into Zoom for his first official kickoff call with Warren. The screen flickered to life, and there he was; mid-50s, square glasses, a bit of a no-nonsense energy. "Morning, Riley," Warren said, nodding. "Glad we've got you on this. We've got a lot to figure out." "Morning, Warren! Excited to help," Riley said. "Tell me what's on your mind." Warren did not hold back. He dove straight in, Oswego City Light had just launched their new website, but the team was still trying to figure out some advanced features.

- Outage Notifications – Their old system sent automated texts to customers, but the new one? They weren't sure how to fully integrate it.

- Self-Service Forms – The public kept getting confused by certain service request forms. Warren needed a way to make them easier to use.

- Staff Training – His internal team wasn't confident using the new website yet—they were constantly emailing him for help.

Riley took notes. Old Riley would have immediately started troubleshooting. But New Riley? New Riley knew that before he fixed anything, he needed to understand the bigger picture.

As Warren talked, Riley felt his instincts kick in. "What would Michael do?" Michael would be patient. Michael would be thoughtful. Michael would make sure Warren felt taken care of. But then, Riley caught himself. "Wait."

"I know what Michael would do... but how would I do

it?" For the first time, he realized: Michael's way wasn't a script. It was a philosophy. And now? It was time for Riley to make it his own.

Riley pulled up a shared doc. "Alright, Warren—here's what I think. Instead of tackling these one at a time, let's put together a structured plan. That way, we don't just fix the issues—we make sure your team feels confident using everything moving forward." Warren raised an eyebrow. "A plan, huh?" "Yep. Here's what I'm thinking."

## Step 1: Outage Notifications Fix

- Riley would walk Warren's team through the integration process and create a simple trouble-shooting guide for them to reference.

## Step 2: Improving the Forms

- Riley would analyze real user behavior, figure out where customers were getting stuck, and mock up a cleaner layout.

- He'd send a Loom video walking Warren through the proposed changes.

## Step 3: Staff Confidence Training

- Instead of just answering questions, Riley would schedule a live training session for Warren's internal team.

- He'd record it so they could reference it later.

He leaned back. "What do you think?" Warren sat there for a moment, rubbing his chin.

"That's... actually really solid. We don't just patch things up, we fix them for the long run." He nodded. "I like how you think, Riley." Riley grinned. "Thanks, Warren. I just want to make sure this works for you; not just today, but long term." Warren let out a small chuckle.

"You know, you remind me of someone." Riley's heart jumped. "Oh yeah?" "Yeah. A guy named Michael. Ever heard of him?" Riley laughed. "Yeah. I've heard of him." Warren smirked. "Well, whatever he did, it worked. Keep doing your version of it." And that's when it hit Riley. He wasn't chasing Michael's legacy anymore. He was building his own.

That evening, Riley closed his laptop, leaned back, and let it all sink in. For weeks, he had measured himself against Michael. Tried to match his tone. Tried to emulate his approach.

Tried to live up to the legend. But today? Warren hadn't said, You're just like Michael. He had said, keep doing your version of it. And for the first time, Riley realized, that was enough. He didn't have to be Michael. He just had to be Riley. And that? That was exactly the kind of technical support specialist he was meant to be.

# CHAPTER 10

# Perfecting the Craft – The Training Challenge

*The Training Session – 3 Hours on Zoom*

Riley exhaled, rolling his shoulders as he checked the clock. Three minutes until the training session started. This wasn't just any training session. This was a full CMS walkthrough for Burnside Electric Association.

And at the other end of the Zoom call?

Max. The main contact at Burnside Electric. The guy who was about to be responsible for updating their website once it launched. And Riley already had a feeling... Max wasn't comfortable with this.

The meeting started, and seven people were on the call, a mix of Burnside Electric employees. Most of them were muted. Cameras off. Riley wasn't surprised. "Alright, good morning everyone!" Riley said, keeping his tone light, warm, engaging. "I know three hours of training might sound like a lot, but I promise; we'll make it fun. Well... at least as fun as managing a website can be, right?" A couple of chuckles. But Max? Max was silent. His camera was off. His microphone muted. Riley smiled. Challenge accepted.

Before going further in, Riley made a mental note that he had to break the silence. "Before we dive in, let's do a quick check; who here has worked with a content management system before?" Silence. Riley chuckled. "Okay, okay, so either no one has, or you're just seeing if I can handle the awkward pause. I see what's happening here." More chuckles.

Then, Max's mic finally clicked on. "I, uh... I've used WordPress a little." Riley jumped on it.

"Ah, WordPress! Nice! Okay, that's actually great news because there are a lot of similarities. Think of this CMS like WordPress but customized for Burnside Electric's needs, so no unnecessary clutter, just the tools you actually need." Max nodded. Camera still off. But at least now he was engaged.

Thirty minutes in, they reached a crucial point in the training, how to edit homepage alerts. Riley shared his screen, walking them through how to update emergency messages. "Alright, that's how it works! Max, why don't you give it a try on your end?" Silence. Then, slowly, Max's camera turned on. He looked tense. "Uh... okay. Let me see."

Riley watched as Max hesitated, clicking around the CMS. His mouse hovered over the settings. But he wasn't clicking. He was stuck. He just didn't want to say it.

Riley thought of Michael. Michael would be patient. Michael would be kind. Michael would make sure Max felt comfortable. But Riley also knew he wasn't Michael. He had to find his own way. So instead of rushing to explain again, Riley paused.

"Hey Max, I can see you're right there in the settings, nice! But before you click, I have a rule I like to use for anyone learning a new system." Max looked at him. "It's called the 'Worst-Case Scenario Rule.' Any guesses what that means?" Max raised an eyebrow. "Uh... that if I mess this up, it's going to be a disaster?" Riley laughed. "Nope! It means that even if you do something wrong, nothing will break permanently. Worst-case scenario? You call me, and we fix it. And best-case scenario? You learn something new today." Max exhaled. Then clicked. And just like that, he updated the alert. "Hey! Look at that, it worked!" Riley said. Max sat back, looking visibly relieved. "That actually wasn't so bad." Riley grinned. "Told you. And hey, remember the rule. If something ever does go wrong, we're here. You're not in this alone."

After that moment, Max was different. His camera stayed on. He asked questions. He even started answering for others. When another Burnside team member asked, "Wait, how do I edit footer links again?" It wasn't Riley who answered. It was Max. "Oh, I got this one! You just go to 'Navigation' and then 'Footer Links', right?" Riley grinned. "Boom. Max, you might be taking over my job soon." More laughs. And now, Max wasn't just learning. He was confident.

As the training wrapped up, Riley pulled up one final slide. "Alright, so before we wrap, just one last thing." On the slide was a single sentence. "You don't have to remember everything today. You just have to remember we're here." Max smiled. "I appreciate that, Riley. I really do." "Good. Because we're not just here for training, we're here long-term. And Max, I have a feeling you're going to be the go-to guy for your team."

Max smirked. "We'll see about that." "No pressure, but I expect you to be running next year's training." Laughter. The session ended. And as Riley closed out of Zoom, he felt something click inside him. This wasn't about getting through a training. It was about giving people the confidence to succeed. And that? That was something he could own.

That night, Riley thought back to the training session. The hesitation. The breakthrough. The way Max grew in confidence right in front of him. Michael had been a huge inspiration. But today? Riley hadn't just done it the Michael way. He had done it his way. And that? That felt like the next step forward.

# CHAPTER 11

# The Future of Client Relationships

*The Final Call with Warren – The End of One Journey, The Start of Another*

Riley logged into Zoom for what would be his final scheduled call with Warren from Oswego City Light. It had been two weeks since they kicked off the project.

- The Outage Notifications were fully integrated.
- The Self-Service Forms had been redesigned for clarity.
- The Staff Training had gone so well that Warren's team had started helping each other before even reaching out to Riley.

And now? Warren didn't need Riley anymore. But that was the whole point.

The screen flickered, and Warren appeared, arms crossed, looking relaxed in a way Riley hadn't seen before. "Well, Riley," Warren said with a smirk. "Looks like you put yourself out of a job."

Riley laughed. "Yeah, well, if I did my job right, you shouldn't need me every day."

Warren nodded. "That's the thing—I know you're still here if we do. That's what matters."

Riley felt a surge of pride. This wasn't just support. This was trust.

Warren leaned forward. "I gotta say—this whole process? It reminded me a little of Michael."

Riley grinned. "You know, I keep hearing that guy's name."

Warren chuckled. "Yeah, well, whatever he did—it stuck. And whatever you're doing? Keep it up."

The call ended.

And Riley sat there for a moment, staring at the empty screen. Michael had set the standard. But today? Riley had built something of his own.

# The Quiet Reflection

It was late.

The glow of Riley's laptop screen was the only light in the room, casting soft blue shadows against the walls. His inbox was finally empty. His Slack notifications were quiet. And yet—he wasn't in a rush to shut everything down. He sat back, stretching his arms, feeling the satisfying weight of a full, productive day.

On his screen, a nearly finished training document sat open—a guide for new clients, breaking down website best practices in plain, easy-to-follow language. He hadn't been asked to write it. No deadline. No pressure. But he had started it because he wanted to. Because he knew it would help people. Because he had finally stopped thinking, "What would Michael do?" And started thinking, "How can I do this in a way that feels like me?"

Riley glanced at the time. 5:42 p.m. A year ago, he would have been counting the minutes until he could log off.

Now? He wasn't just working support. He wasn't just fixing tickets. He was teaching, mentoring, building relationships. He was helping people feel confident, capable, taken care of. And for the first time, he let himself fully admit it: "I love this."

He smiled, closed his laptop, and leaned back in his chair. Michael had been the inspiration. But Riley had found his own way. And the best part? He was just getting started.

# The End

Final Thought.

This isn't just the end of Riley's story. It's the beginning of a new standard; one that's still being written.

**The Michael Standard lives on.**

And now?

So does Riley's.

# About the Author

Charlie Stanley is the CEO of Powerful, a company dedicated to thoughtful, intentional, and purpose-driven service for utility organizations. His leadership philosophy is rooted in the belief that exceptional customer experiences aren't just about solving problems—they're about building trust, fostering meaningful relationships, and turning customers into raving fans.

Inspired by Raving Fans by Ken Blanchard and Sheldon Bowles, Charlie set out to redefine what great service looks like. Under his leadership, Powerful has earned national recognition as a standout workplace, being named in Newsweek's Top 100 Most Loved Workplaces in America and Inc.'s Best Workplaces. The Oregonian ranked Powerful as the No. 1 Top Workplace in 2024 for companies under 100 employees, and the Portland Business Journal named it the No. 2 Best Place to Work in Oregon and Southwest Washington in 2023. Additionally, Inc. Magazine recognized Powerful with its

Best in Business and Power Partner Awards, and the company was honored with the Better Business Bureau Torch Award for Ethics.

Charlie believes that true success comes from serving with intention, leading with integrity, and always putting people first. Through this book, he hopes to inspire others to embrace a more thoughtful approach to customer experience—one that creates loyalty, trust, and lasting impact. His passion for service excellence extends beyond his work, as he is constantly fascinated by ways to enhance and humanize customer experiences.

An avid traveler, Charlie has visited 49 states and 17 countries, always eager to explore new places and gain fresh perspectives. When he's not leading his team or championing great service, he enjoys traveling and spending time with his dog, Nitro.